trending + timeless baby names

FROM THE NAME MENTOR

@namesdaily

*xo
Alix*

how to use this book

I set out a really long time ago to be different. I changed my destiny, I wove deeply into myself the things that kept my soul on fire. I took the fences down around my heart, and made way for the river. I decided I would rather be overtaken by things begun in love, even if they didn't end how I'd imagined, than live a life with boundaries determined by other people.

I wasn't always so in love with freedom and this idea of being myself. For a long time I let other people sit in my saddle and I got roped into a lot of decisions that pained me. I learned along the way that I'm the sea captain of my own story, and it's better to go down with a ship full of treasure than be robbed of the joy and peace of passion and purpose.

And I'll tell you, nothing taught me more about this than motherhood.

This isn't a traditional name book. I didn't want to hand you another name dictionary. I wanted to hand you a compass that led you to the conclusion of what you actually want and believe. You'll find 50 boy names and 50 girl names, paired 20 different ways to give you a spark. And while I believe the names in here are timeless beauties, I hope that this book helps you decide even if these names aren't for you and what you like.

Whatever is keeping you from going with your gut and breaking open the things in your heart, I lovingly hope it gets put to rest by the end of these pages.

xo, Alix

#name mentor

4

These beauties were some of the mothers
I was lucky enough to grow up with.

table of contents

how to use this book
pages 4-5

girl names
pages 8-59

boy names
pages 70-121

how to build a name
pages 62-63

first names first + middle names
pages 64-65

the seat of honor
pages 66-67

when it comes down to it
pages 68-69

acknowledgements
pages 122-123

"Words are things. You must be careful, careful about calling people out of their names... Some day we'll be able to measure the power of words. I think they are things. They get on the walls. They get in your wallpaper. They get in your rugs, in your upholstery, and your clothes, and finally, into you."

— Maya Angelou

meet the name mentor

Coffee sipper.
Kindness preacher.
Uneven hoodie strings fixer.
Instagram's 1st namer.

I've been in love with the power of names my whole life. I started out blogging, then moved into YouTube, and eventually found my heart strings in Instagram where I was lucky enough to be the first official account for names. Interfacing with people, sharing moments and milestones in their lives, well, it's humbling, inspiring, and it's led me to experience a whole lot of naming. Look, I named my own little girl, I know. It can be frightening enough to make you pee your pants. (Or at least when you laugh now.)

/thenamementor @namesdaily
thenamementor.com

hey girl hey

Who will your daughter be? How do you capture what your heart is wishing for her, all while having no idea what her own thoughts are? Maybe, just maybe, your own heart knows the answer, and maybe that's why you have drawn the line across so many names already.

If you thought Elvis and Regis were the only peeps who could be known by their first names, then let's remember Adele and Beyoncé. Names that have become permanently bonded with power, talent, and beauty.

But how does one name a daughter? There's this being whom you have so much hope and deep heart-pangs for. Maybe for freedom, self-confidence, and bringing about change, or knowing her worth against the odds that you hope don't break her wondrous heart.

When giving your daughter a name, I think we want her to know what she's made of. We want it to be inspirational or aspirational, maybe, letting her know of the powerful women who have gone before her. We want it to be happy. We want it to be diamond quality and cruelty-free. We want it to fit right and stand out. No pressure, right? :P

These next fifty names were curated with the intention of being fun, brilliant, beautiful, and classy names for you to easily digest. Names that could live across a lot of lifetimes, and not be too heavy to carry around in a wild and wonderful youth.

Congratulations on your girl!

— Alix, the name mentor

Betsy

The name Betsy has such an upbeat sound. It's fun while grounded.
If you love the sight of wildflowers, wishing wells and antique shops,
you'll love this name. It's vintage cute.

Some pairing ideas

Betsy Pearl	Moira Betsy
Betsy Nola	Zinnea Betsy
Betsy Nora/Norah	Lula Betsy
Betsy Isabelle	Jewel Betsy
Betsy Violet	Della Betsy
Betsy Odessa	Teagan Betsy
Betsy Willa	Willa Betsy
Betsy Winter	Iona Betsy
Betsy Aurora	Georgia Betsy
Betsy June	Flora Betsy

meaning

pronounced bet-see | pledged to God | comes from the name Elizabeth
English
#namesdailybetsy

Collins

The name Collins hit a homerun when she starred in *The Blind Side*.
She's cute while feeling she can still roll up her sleeves and do it well.
She's sassy and classy and is begging for the nickname CeCe or
Coco. Or Collie. Or Clio. Somebody stop me...

some pairing ideas

Nora Collins	Collins Odessa
Maisie Collins	Collins Olivia/Alivia
Susie/Suzie Collins	Collins Winter
Brenna Collins	Collins Maisie
Lucy Collins	Collins Piper
Gemma Collins	Collins Felicity
Liv Collins	Collins Jovie
Jovie Collins	Collins Miranda
Haddie Collins	Collins Magnolia
Primrose Collins	Collins Jade

meaning

pronounced kahl-linz | darling, term of endearment for a young hound,
descendent of a warrior, or the people's victory
Irish, English
#namesdailycollins

Evelyn

The name Evelyn is that of poetry and prose. Have you read the one from Robert Browning? He says she's made of "spirit, fire and dew." I couldn't have summed it up better. But here I go! Evelyn is made of sugar, deep roots and um, fire and dew. Nicknames? Evie and Elvi!

some pairing ideas

Evelyn Merritt
Evelyn Rosalie
Evelyn Margot/Margaux
Evelyn Holiday
Evelyn James
Evelyn Grey/Gray
Evelyn Tindra
Evelyn Genevieve
Evelyn Winona
Evelyn Carys

Isla Evelyn
Junie Evelyn
Heidi Evelyn
Frances Evelyn
Frankie Evelyn
Reese Evelyn
Norah Evelyn
Mary Evelyn
Keira Evelyn
Dahlia Evelyn

meaning

pronounced ev-uh-lin | wished-for child
English, German
#namesdailyevelyn

Vesper

The name Vesper is lyrical and hauntingly beautiful. Makes you want to whisper a song. It feels a little exotic with the genuity of the ancients. It has this longing that gets my creativity excited. Some inspiring qualities, right?

some pairing ideas

Vesper Belle	Lillian Vesper
Vesper Rosamund	Bellamy Vesper
Vesper Etta	Isobel Vesper
Vesper Millay	Rosie Vesper
Vesper Constance	Milligan Vesper
Vesper Aléna	Millicent Vesper
Vesper Song	Caroline Vesper
Vesper Lillian	Julia Vesper
Vesper Eulalie	Cecilia Vesper
Vesper Cleo	Selina Vesper

meaning

pronounced vess-per | the evening star,
of or pertaining to the evening
Latin
#namesdailyvesper

Una

The name Una, also spelled Oona, is such a delightful name. Like seriously, how can saying the name Una not make you smile? She could be a hero or a poet or a sweet girl in a bonnet. (I have a love for bonnets.) She is darling.

some pairing ideas

Una Scarlet	Adelaide Una
Una Coralie	Kate Una
Una Frances	Sonnet Una
Una Holiday	Vesper Una
Una Brave	Violet Una
Una Fae/Fay	Elodie Una
Una Maple	Penelope Una
Una Melody	Harper Una
Una Margot	Zoey Una
Una Lucille	Daisy Una

meaning

pronounced oo-nuh | lamb | one
Irish, Scottish
#namesdailyuna

14

Sally

The name Sally is written on my own heart, so I can't help but talk it up. It's vintage cute. She can follow it through nursery rhymes all the way to big city lights. She's simple but sweet, quiet but happy, old but timeless and sincere.

some pairing ideas

Sally Meadow	Faegan Sally
Sally Blythe	Fiona Sally
Sally Golden	Cora Sally
Sally Cosima	Harper Sally
Sally Juniper	Arden Sally
Sally Margaret	Avia Sally
Sally James	Tatum Sally
Sally Marigold	Winslow Sally
Sally Winslet	Merritt Sally
Sally Blue	Phaedra Sally

meaning

pronounced sal-lee | princess
English
#namesdailysally

Cassia

If you're a biblical sort, cassia is a cinnamon spice that was one of the seven spices used in incense. It's the bark taken off of the cassia tree. It has a beautiful, fragrant sound as well, almost a princess name with a little bit of that exotic flair.

some pairing ideas

Cassia Melody	Vera Cassia
Cassia Grey	Halle Cassia
Cassia Justice	Sloane Cassia
Cassia Gwen	Ione Cassia
Cassia Raelynn	Bex Cassia
Cassia Bonnie	Ember Cassia
Cassia Wynne	Margaret Cassia
Cassia Quinn	Emmie Cassia
Cassia Vané	Millicent Cassia
Cassia Rumi	Evie Cassia

meaning

pronounced cass-ee-uh & cash-uh | cinnamon from the cassia tree
Ancient Hebrew
#namesdailycassia

Junia

She's an ancient name with an elegance. She's meant for prose
and the delicate, deep meaning of spectacular things.
Junie is a really pretty nickname.

some pairing ideas

Junia Pearl	Marigold Junia
Junia Wren	Reagan Junia
Junia Reagan	Fox Junia
Junia Violet	Rosie Junia
Junia Lisette	Winnie Junia
Junia Collins	Lorelai Junia
Junia Faye	Coco Junia
Junia James	Tannen Junia
Junia Soul	Beatrix Junia
Junia Sky	Winter Junia

meaning

pronounced joo-nee-uh | youth, youthful | born in June
Ancient Hebrew, Latin
#namesdailyjunia

Lillian

It has its roots in flora and classic country music. That makes it perfect in
my book. And because this name is so tried and true, it is prime to be
paired with an unexpected and edgy name.
Besides the nickname Lily, there's Lilla, Lilia and Lenni.

some pairing ideas

Lillian Piper	Ivy Lillian
Lillian Reese	Greta Lillian
Lillian Vesper	Caro Lillian
Lillian Coco	Briar Lillian
Lillian Grey	Patsy Lillian
Lillian Charlotte	Ever Lillian
Lillian Bee	Aidy Lillian
Lillian Phayre	Cora Lillian
Lillian True	James Lillian
Lillian Georgia	Brave Lillian

meaning

pronounced lilly-in | lily, pure
Latin
#namesdailylillian

Juniper

I grew up in the mountains and juniper was everywhere, their familial system holding the rocky cliff edges together. Happy and constant. Made into arrows and baskets, their berries are treasured healers. As Ed Sheeran said: "Honey, your soul could never grow old, it's evergreen."

some pairing ideas

Juniper Bly	Winnie Juniper
Juniper Elle	Elle Juniper
Juniper Eisley	Miley Juniper
Juniper Farrow	Faye Juniper
Juniper Isla	Reeva Juniper
Juniper Enya	Mary Juniper
Juniper Maisie	Zoe Juniper
Juniper Adele	Lyra Juniper
Juniper Arlo	Nelle Juniper
Juniper Corliss	Maddie Juniper

meaning

pronounced joo-nih-per | youth producing | evergreen
from Latin
#namesdailyjuniper

Winslow

Winslow sounds like a cozy knitted scarf with a book in a coffee shop. Winslow also sounds like a mountain painter and a glass ceiling breaker. There is something about this name that is majestic, artistic, and warm.

some pairing ideas

Winslow Daphne	Emma Winslow
Winslow Daisy	Caia Winslow
Winslow Annie	Sadie Winslow
Winslow Simone	Journey Winslow
Winslow Cate	Birdie Winslow
Winslow Ree	Piper Winslow
Winslow Camille	Harper Winslow
Winslow Ruby	Raven Winslow
Winslow Rebecca	Micah Winslow
Winslow Poppy	Grace Winslow

meaning

pronounced winz-low | hill belonging to wine | friend's hill
Old English

#namesdailywinslow

Sonnet

Seamus Heaney said "Sonnet is about movement in a form." We feel the baby growing inside of us, their hiccups, their kicks - we give them life and they give us ours. There is beauty in the often unnoticed, and power when we take notice. The minor is major.

some pairing ideas

Sonnet Ellowyn	Everly Sonnet
Sonnet Shakespeare	Tekla Sonnet
Sonnet Adele	Malina Sonnet
Sonnet Briann	Milla Sonnet
Sonnet Vivienne	Myla Sonnet
Sonnet Jasper	Felicity Sonnet
Sonnet Meagan	Josephine Sonnet
Sonnet Keziah	Phaedra Sonnet
Sonnet Kerenza	Julianna Sonnet
Sonnet Emberly	Rowan Sonnet

meaning

pronounced sahn-nit | little song | short lyrical poem
Italian, Middle French
#namesdailysonnet

Winona

When I say Winona, I can feel a breeze on my face from across the prairie.
I feel a strength and a charisma with a wild beauty.

some pairing ideas

Winona Pearl	Birdie Winona
Winona Brave	Scout Winona
Winona Violet	Tess Winona
Winona Maggie	Dottie Winona
Winona Mae	Maisie Winona
Winona Scarlet	Lucy Winona
Winona Sparrow	Audrey Winona
Winona Fox	Betsy Winona
Winona Aubrey	Francie Winona
Winona Birdie	Hadley Winona

meaning

pronounced wih-no-nuh | firstborn daughter
Dakota, Sioux
#namesdailywinona

Kate + Cate

I adore the name John. It is so classic and strong, it's well-rounded and has a certain "I've known you all my life" appeal. To me, Kate/Cate is exactly that way. It's hard to pin down which era they're from. So beautiful and sweet to say.

some pairing ideas

Kate Indigo	Winter Kate
Kate Evalince	Vesper Kate
Cate Ione Winter	Brinley Kate
Cate Tessa Blair	Harlow Kate
Kate Tallulah	Bellamy Kate
Cate Beatrix	Juniper Cate
Cate Vesper	Luella Kate
Kate Winona	Tenley Kate
Kate Magnolia	Wilder Kate
Cate Winslow	Ever Kate

meaning

pronounced cait | pure
English

#namesdailykate   #namesdailycate

Cecelia

Oh, love is blind. It's also strong and caring and kind and trail-blazing.
Don't let the meaning of this name stump you.
All children are born blind; hate and kindness are learned.
Nicknames? Cece, Lele, Lia, Celie. (Some also spell this Cecilia.)

some pairing ideas

Cecelia Violet	Arlo Cecelia
Cecelia Blair	Marlowe Cecelia
Cecelia Tate	Wren Cecelia
Cecelia Margot	Penny Cecelia
Cecelia Fox	Bonnie Cecelia
Cecelia Moore	Vesper Cecelia
Cecelia Anwen	Blair Cecelia
Cecelia Harper	Conley Cecelia
Cecelia Wilde	Rooney Cecelia
Cecelia Quinn	Birdie Cecelia

meaning

pronounced seh-seel-yuh | blind
Latin
#namesdailycecelia

Birdie

"The bird dares to break the shell, then the shell breaks open
and the bird can fly openly. This is the simplest principle of success.
You dream, you dare and you fly." - *Israelmore Ayivor*
"Oh, bird of my soul, fly away now, For I possess a hundred fortified towers." - *Rumi*

some pairing ideas

Birdie Magnolia	Bex Birdie
Birdie Jessamine	Nala Birdie
Birdie Margaret	Madelyn Birdie
Birdie Hazel	Isla Birdie
Birdie Lorelai	Rosalind Birdie
Birdie Tindra	Sutton Birdie
Birdie Faegan	Helena Birdie
Birdie Zosia	Skyler Birdie
Birdie Victoria	Lula Birdie
Birdie Aurelia	Kasha Birdie

meaning

pronounced burr-dee | little bird
English
#namesdailybirdie

Faegan

I see fairies and forests and lanterns. This name lights up a room!
Fae and Fin are super cute nicknames!

some pairing ideas

Faegan Odessa
Faegan Moira
Faegan Daphne
Faegan Drew
Faegan Tigerlily
Faegan Auora
Faegan Esme
Faegan Isla
Faegan Merritt
Faegan Rory

Rory Faegan
Marlowe Faegan
Violet Faegan
Tilly Faegan
Birdie Faegan
Tessa Faegan
Ruby Faegan
Elinore Faegan
Rilla Faegan
Etta Faegan

meaning

pronounced fay-gin | joyful
English, Irish
#namesdailyfaegan

26

Tindra

When I first heard this name, I swooned. In fact, Tindra was the very first post I made on @namesdaily. All these years later, I'm still just as excited about it. This is a rare gem.

some pairing ideas

Tindra Naomi	Harlow Tindra
Tindra Violet	Sybil Tindra
Tindra Diamond	Willow Tindra
Tindra Melody	Cami Tindra
Tindra Poet	Fox Tindra
Tindra Belle	Arrow Tindra
Tindra Sadie	Bo Tindra
Tindra Winter	Ruthie Tindra
Tindra Sophie	Gem Tindra
Tindra Adelaide	Alessia Tindra

meaning

pronounced tin-druh | to twinkle or sparkle
Swedish
#namesdailytindra

Elowen + Ellowyn

Hhhhhhhhhh. Gorgeousness. Elle, Ella or Wynnie could be a nickname.
The Cornish language was recently denoted as a true language. With this has come the
discovery of Cornish words, like Elowen, and the Cornish people are using these words
as names to honor their heritage and this new excitement in their language.

Some pairing ideas

Elowen Elise	Juniper Ellowyn
Ellowyn Reese	Maggie Elowen
Elowen Charlotte	Merit Ellowyn
Elowen Ruby	Briony Elowen
Elowen Lux	Casper Ellowyn
Elowen Fern	Junie Elowen
Elowen Maeve	Autumn Elowen
Elowen Dorothy	Poet Elowen
Elowen Jovie	Lark Elowen
Elowen Reverie	Aoki Ellowyn

meaning

pronounced el-low-in | elm tree
Cornish

#namesdailyelowen   #namesdailyellowyn

Cleo + Clio

A name that ends in -o is bound to be fun. Maybe because of Cleopatra,
it has that "taken seriously" element to it that adds to the charm.
It's short but lilting, strong but fun.

some pairing ideas

Cleo Wren	Winslet Cleo
Cleo Ivy	London Clio
Cleo Sunday	Dove Clio
Cleo Remington	Nolwenn Cleo
Cleo Nasrin	Cambrie Cleo
Cleo Valentina	Rosamund Clio
Cleo Jackie	Emerson Clio
Cleo Briar	Milligan Cleo
Cleo Diana	River Cleo
Clio Penelope	Audrey Clio

meaning

pronounced clee-oh | glory, illustrious
Greek

#namesdailycleo   #namesdailyclio

Reese

You hear the name Reese and you go, "Wow, that sounds like someone fun to be around!" Sweet and sure, friendly and straightforward.

some pairing ideas

Reese Melody
Reese Fiona
Reese Maud
Reese Penelope
Reese Viola
Reese Winslet
Reese Ivy
Reese Juliet
Reese Winslow
Reese Georgia

Lillian Reese
Lyla Reese
Tessa Reese, always
Bay Reese
Aspen Reese
Elowyn Reese
Quinn Reese
Avia Reese
Winona Reese
Julia Reese

meaning

pronounced rees | ardor, enthusiasm, fiery
Welsh
#namesdailyreese

Margot + Margaux

It feels like a sister spirit to Jo March, but also could be a cool queen.
Regal but fun. Sprinkled with vintage charm but also fashion.
I feel like if Audrey Hepburn shared her name list
with us, Margot would be on it.

some pairing ideas

Margot Sky	Robbie Margot, obvs
Margot Ella	Piper Margot
Margot Adela	Jetta Margot
Margot Briony	Ivy Margot
Margot Alexa	Lilia Margot
Margot Fox	Ella Margot
Margot River	Jula Margot
Margot June	Elsa Margot
Margot Ree	Milla Margot
Margot Augusta	Miller Margot

meaning

pronounced mar-go | pearl
French

#namesdailymargot   #namesdailymargaux

Kina + Kinah

A name that is as darling and daring as a pixie cut. I love how
its shortness adds to its sweetness. It's a name you're surprised to
hear but something you quickly love to say.

some pairing ideas

Kina Scarlet	Zoe Kinah
Kina Rosalie	Rory Kinah
Kina Winter	Violet Kinah
Kina Ember	Moonie Kina
Kinah Free	Sparrow Kinah
Kina Harper	Raven Kina
Kinah Brave	Ever Kinah
Kinah Oceane	Aidy Kina
Kina Liv	Joslyn Kina
Kinah Juniper	Arwen Kina

meaning

pronounced kee-nuh | China | strong-willed
Hawaiian, Hebrew
#namesdailykina   #namesdailykinah

Pearl

There's something about pearls that captivates us as people. This treasure, created in the sea, a delicate jewel of process that we string together and wear for the glory of passing it on. Pearl is truly something old, something new, and something borrowed.

some pairing ideas

Pearl Hathaway	Indie Pearl
Pearl Milligan	Carys Pearl
Pearl Gloria	Millicent Pearl
Pearl Noelle	Odessa Pearl
Pearl Josephine	Una Pearl
Pearl Gwendolyn	Esme Pearl
Pearl Odessa	Susannah Pearl
Pearl Evangeline	Emmeth Pearl
Pearl Winona	Arlowe Pearl
Pearl Imogen	Ebony Pearl

meaning

pronounced purl | a semi-precious gemstone
Latin
n a m e s d a i l y p e a r l

Susan

She's a dark-eyed flower that stood for women's rights.
She wears a pink ribbon and lives in Narnia. What a name!
She has that soft "-in" ending that is so endearing.
If you want a newer-sounding nickname, think of Sunny!

some pairing ideas

Susan Wilder	Ellanore Susan
Susan Marlowe	Briony Susan
Susan Briar	Marigold Susan
Susan Maple	Golda Susan
Susan Harper	Story Susan
Susan Winter	Parker Susan
Susan Collins	Coco Susan
Susan Meg	Annie Susan
Susan Caro	Kelleth Susan
Susan Willow	Briar Susan

meaning

pronounced soo-zin | lily
English
#namesdailysusan

34

Saskia

Saskia - made of magic and mystery and strength.
She's an armful of wildflowers and the captain of her own ship.
She fills the pages of her life with tales of valor and the soft
ways of kindness. She filled up my own girlhood with wonder.

some pairing ideas

Saskia Wren	Blair Saskia
Saskia Lark	Cate Saskia
Saskia True	Elvi Saskia
Saskia Emme	Evie Saskia
Saskia Blaire	Anouk Saskia
Saskia Gem	Ivy Saskia
Saskia Bennett	Valley Saskia
Saskia Wynne	Florrie Saskia
Saskia Winter	Goldie Saskia
Saskia Meadow	Wilder Saskia

meaning

pronounced soss-kee-uh | saxon | knife | protector of mankind
Dutch, Slavic
#namesdailysaskia

Holiday

Holiday seems caught up in the smoky glam of Old Hollywood. She's got the voice to stand out, and she's the soft glittering lights of Christmas by the fire. Warm, friendly, and full of life. Your child's birth is a holiday!

some pairing ideas

Holiday Susan	Winnie Holiday
Holiday Gwen	Ella Holiday
Holiday Fern	Ember Holiday
Holiday Maxwell	Caia Holiday
Holiday Quinn	Juna Holiday
Holiday Charlotte	Roman Holiday, yes please
Holiday Nora	Neva Holiday
Holiday Emma	Jackie Holiday
Holiday Brenna	Tessa Holiday
Holiday Roisin	Bonnie Holiday

meaning

pronounced hahl-ih-day | born on a holy day
English
#namesdailyholiday

Margaret

Margaret has adorned royalty, celebs, authors, and other prominent people since medieval times. And yet, she also seems like a close, down-to-earth best friend. She seems like an ancient castle in the woods, a warm hug, a favorite book, and a glorious outlook.

some pairing ideas

Margaret Fox	Nelle Margaret
Margaret Norah	Calla Margaret
Margaret Sylvie	Wren Margaret
Margaret Rosalie	Junie Margaret
Margaret Adele	Cecily Margaret
Margaret Honor	Claire Margaret
Margaret Wilde	Bly Margaret
Margaret Aspen	Rooney Margaret
Margaret Willa	Sailor Margaret
Margaret Blossom	Posey Margaret

meaning

pronounced mar-grit | pearl
Medieval, Greek
#namesdailymargaret

Zosia

She's the Polish version of Sophie/Sophia. I was a lucky girl to have a Polish grandmother, and her sister was Zosia. When I picture Zosia, I see strength and blue cornflowers, a busy kitchen, and heritage. She's so fun, and Zo is a really rad nickname.

some pairing ideas

Zosia Caroline	Winsley Zosia
Zosia Camille	Guinevere Zosia
Zosia Winter	August Zosia
Zosia Blue	Haven Zosia
Zosia Katarina	Scarlett Zosia
Zosia Love	Mary Zosia
Zosia Mary	Rumi Zosia
Zosia May	Katie Zosia
Zosia Emmeline	Kadie Zosia
Zosia Isabelle	Belle Zosia

meaning

pronounced zoh-shuh | wisdom
Polish
#namesdailyzosia

Evalince

It has the sparkle of evanescence, yet the solidity of Evelyn. There is not much known about this name, which means it can only go up! I love the nickname Elvi for this!

some pairing ideas

Evalince Mary	Piper Evalince
Evalince Opal	Aidy Evalince
Evalince Aurora	Halley Evalince
Evalince Rue	Nola Evalince
Evalince Piper	Joni Evalince
Evalince Aoki	Cara Evalince
Evalince India	Bee Evalince
Evalince Velvet	Fern Evalince
Evalince Ada	Lydia Evalince
Evalince Ree	Lou Evalince

meaning

pronounced ev-uh-lince | wished-for child | life
origin uncertain
#namesdailyevalince

Linden

It's soft, sweet, and yet presidential.
"The wind, with a sway and rustle, Toss'd the leaves of the linden tree,
And, deep in the silvery shadow, A treasure was shown to me."
- Eliza Craven Green

Some pairing ideas

Linden Violet	Lark Linden
Linden Snow	Ava Linden
Linden Avery	Mary Linden
Linden Sylvie	Marigold Linden
Linden Greta	Ruby Linden
Linden Aria	Bowie Linden
Linden Jackie	Tessa Linden
Linden Phayre	Rory Linden
Linden Cora	Cora Linden
Linden Ramona	Romy Linden

meaning

pronounced lin-din | lime tree hill
English
#namesdailylinden

Maren

Growing up with horses, I love how this is a nod to horse lovers.
She's a wistful and winsome Mary who now can write a pretty
amazing song and croon deep enough to touch your heart.
When the moon hits your eye, reflects the sea and the sky, it's a Maren...

some pairing ideas

Maren Patsy	Blythe Maren
Maren Birdie	Bowie Maren
Maren Odessa	Golda Maren
Maren Elizabeth	Willow Maren
Maren Alexa	Lennox Maren
Maren Adelaide	Isle Maren
Maren Gemma	Winter Maren
Maren Violet	Olive Maren
Maren Meadow	Ivy Maren
Maren Olivia	Emmeth Maren

meaning

pronounced mair-in | sea
Latin
#namesdailymaren

Etta

Etta sounds so full of soul. It's so beautiful and has this strange power in its simplicity and style. I envision Etta like a bright coral lipstick. No, it's not the traditional and classic red, or a trendy color... it just simply makes a statement without being a statement.

some pairing ideas

Etta Margot	Why not Henry Etta???
Etta Pearl	Emberly Etta
Etta Marian	Liesel Etta
Etta Marianne	Briony Etta
Etta Maria	Solene Etta
Etta Sky	Mirabelle Etta
Etta Moon	Bellamy Etta
Etta Grey	Margalo Etta
Etta Rosalie	Casper Etta
Etta Mirabelle	Roan Etta

meaning

pronounced et-tuh | ruler of the home | little one | pearl
Scottish, German, Greek
#namesdailyetta

Felicity

"Seek not greater wealth, but simpler pleasure; not higher fortune,
but deeper felicity." - *Mahatma Gandhi*
"A win for one is a win for all - and I'm not just saying that
because Dumas did." - *Felicity Huffman*

some pairing ideas

Felicity Wren	Luella Felicity
Felicity Jane	Sawyer Felicity
Felicity Juliet	Isla Felicity
Felicity Cora	Cora Felicity
Felicity Norah	Adeline Felicity
Felicity Gwen	Rosalind Felicity
Felicity Winter	Keira Felicity
Felicity Ella	Tannen Felicity
Felicity Jade	Tindra Felicity
Felicity Belle	Gemma Felicity

meaning

pronounced fuh-liss-iddy | good fortune, happy
Latin
#namesdailyfelicity

Isla

Isla feels like a beach party while simultaneously ruling an empire in style.
Fun, bubbly, spunky, talented, creative, and determined.
Wait, did I just describe Isla Fisher???

some pairing ideas

Isla Josephine	Moore Isla
Isla Rune	Rose Isla
Isla Oceane	Daphne Isla
Isla Cheyenne	Fern Isla
Isla Juliet	Zoe Isla
Isla Rose	Brynn Isla
Isla Maegan	Cassidy Isla
Isla Farrow	Rumor Isla
Isla Julienne	Cece Isla
Isla Vivian	Brighton Isla

meaning

pronounced eye-luh | island
Scottish
#namesdailyisla

Tess

A beautiful way to honor a Theresa or Esther.
Tess is so abundant with that feeling of closeness and strength.
A name you can rely on to stand the test of time. Full of beauty,
grace, and a name that's stayed in the underused category.

some pairing ideas

Tess Ophelia	Willow Tess
Tess Annie Blair	Briony Tess
Tess Winslow	Briar Tess
Tess Eliza Primrose	Marigold Tess
Tess Magnolia	Eliza Tess
Tess Aurelia	Calla Junie Tess
Tess Olivia Gray	Winslow Emma Tess
Tess Winona Ruby	Everly Tess
Tess Violet James	Winnie Isla Tess
Tess Willow	Una Tess

meaning

pronounced tess | harvester
English
#namesdailytess

Jette

You could say this is a fly name. Short and sweet but full of personality.
It also has that classy and jazzy Old Hollywood vibe.

some pairing ideas

Jette Alora	Charlie Jette
Jette Milligan	Lorelei Jette
Jette Harper	Emma Bo Jette
Jette Mila	Winnie Ella Jette
Jette Elizabeth	Calla Jette
Jette Claire	Miranda Jette
Jette Harlow	Elsa Jette
Jette Marlowe	Minoux Jette
Jette James	Tenley Jette
Jette Elora	Emberly Jette

meaning

pronounced jet | aircraft | intense black color | a mineral
English
#namesdailyjette

Coralie

Beautiful, oceany, and colorful.

some pairing ideas

Coralie Fox	Winslow Coralie
Coralie June	Della Coralie
Coralie Gwen	James Coralie
Coralie Roux	Penna Coralie
Coralie Guinevere	Sloane Coralie
Coralie Gemma	Meg Coralie
Coralie Emma	Lux Coralie
Coralie Wren	Amada Coralie
Coralie Kate	Sybil Coralie
Coralie Winslow	Quinn Coralie

meaning

pronounced core-uh-lee | coral | little maiden
French
#namesdailycoralie

Goldie

Bright, happy, endeared, cherished, and twinkles in the sunlight.
"I have witnessed the softening of the hardest of hearts by a simple smile."
- Goldie Hawn

some pairing ideas

Goldie Matilda	Maren Goldie
Goldie Emmeth	Reese Goldie
Goldie Raya	Luella Goldie
Goldie Wyatt	Tess Goldie
Goldie Lillian	Brynn Goldie
Goldie Margaret	Brenna Goldie
Goldie Collins	Millicent Goldie
Goldie Faye	River Goldie
Goldie Rebecca	Autumn Goldie
Goldie Tess	Junia Goldie

meaning

pronounced gole-dee | gold, golden | gilded
English
#namesdailygoldie

Rosamund

There is something about this name that catches me when I hear it.
It turns my head and I marvel at what a gem it is. It's both romantic
and fierce, elegant and moody and mysterious. It's meant to
be written down alongside a great and beautiful story.

some pairing ideas

Rosamund Fox
Rosamund River
Rosamund Pike is like the perfect name ever
Rosamund Grey
Rosamund Juliet
Rosamund Moore
Rosamund Violet
Rosamund Pearl
Rosamund Delilah
Rosamund Kate

May Rosamund
Caia Rosamund
Katie Rosamund
Winnie Rosamund
Blake Rosamund
Greer Rosamund
Ardon Rosamund
Mina Rosamund
Cosima Rosamund
Pippa Rosamund

meaning

pronounced rose-uh-mund | horse protection
German
#namesdailyrosamund

Prairie

Lives in storybooks and the home of people who call her a companion.
Full of flowers and seasons, a home to the wind and change.
Queue Dixie Chicks *Wide Open Spaces*. Such a beautiful name.

some pairing ideas

Prairie Winona   Delilah Prairie
Prairie Rae   Ellanore Prairie
Prairie Blue   Wynne Prairie
Prairie Adele   Joan Prairie
Prairie Eliza   Luella Prairie
Prairie Wilder   Emmylou Prairie
Prairie Mattiemae   Miller Prairie
Prairie Ella   Arlo Prairie
Prairie Skya   Arlowe Prairie
Prairie Lark   Frances Prairie

meaning

pronounced prair-ree | grassland, meadow
French
#namesdailyprairie

Marlowe

*"O, thou art fairer than the evening air
clad in the beauty of a thousand stars."*
- Christopher Marlowe

some pairing ideas

Marlowe Aspen	Josie Marlowe
Marlowe Sage	Ava Marlowe
Marlowe Claire	Fox Marlowe
Marlowe Josie	Maggie Marlowe
Marlowe Holiday	Birdie Marlowe
Marlowe Jette	Collins Marlowe
Marlowe Avery	Jade Marlowe
Marlowe Maeve	Audrey Marlowe
Marlowe Song	Aubrey Marlowe
Marlowe Jamie	Ruby Marlowe

meaning

pronounced mar-low | driftwood | marshy meadow
English
#namesdailymarlowe

Winslet

I grew up admiring Kate Winslet, obviously. She is goals, or at least, my goals. Forever ago, I saw a news article online about a brave girl named Winslet, and it deeply impacted me. It stuck out as quite a powerful, whimsical, lyrical, and beautiful name. And did I mention Kate Winslet?

Some pairing ideas

Winslet Faye	Blythe Winslet
Winslet Mary	Kate Winslet for life please
Winslet Rebecca	Margo Winslet
Winslet Caroline	Sage Winslet
Winslet Honor	Molly Winslet
Winslet Mae/May	Rosie Winslet
Winslet Opal	Jula Winslet
Winslet Phayre	Emery Winslet
Winslet Gray	Ember Winslet
Winslet Anne	Una Winslet

meaning

pronounced winz-lit | fair, pure channel or stream
English
#namesdailywinslet

Arden

It seems to be unrelated to the word ardent, but that's what
I always think when I hear this name. As Mr. Darcy said,
"I love you. Most ardently."

some pairing ideas

Arden Winter Sage	Scout Arden
Arden Beatrix	Jewel Arden
Arden Blythe	Vess Arden
Arden Willa Gray	Magnolia Arden
Arden Marigold	Junie Arden
Arden Guinevere	Felicity Arden
Arden Jewel	Penelope Arden
Arden Clio Wren	Faye Arden
Arden Sparrow	Jo Arden
Arden Poppy	Winsley Arden

meaning

pronounced ar-din | high | valley of the eagle
a place of solitude and great beauty
English, Hebrew
#namesdailyarden

Della

If you're wanting a name as rare as the northern lights, and just as
beautiful, here is Della. So gorgeous, right?! And as always, I think
of the deep well of strength that was Della Reese:
"People have known me for so long, I'm just Della to them."

some pairing ideas

Della Reese still sings to my heart
Della Solene
Della Imogen
Della Golden
Della Blue
Della James
Della Kate
Della Ruby
Della Fox
Della Tierney

Eisley Della
Penelope Della
Harper Della
Joni Della
Winter Della
Ruby Della
Charlotte Della
Charlie Della Kate
Junie Della
Ever Della

meaning

pronounced del-luh | a small valley or glen
bright, noble, or of the nobility
Old English
#namesdailydella

Frances

She's graced the stage and classic books, including Jane Austen,
and also fought for women's rights. There's a quiet and gentleness
about Frances that has the same draw to me as a maternal love.
And the nickname Francie is so cute it's ridiculous.

some pairing ideas

Frances Fox	Una Frances
Frances Moore	Winslow Frances
Frances Meadow	Scarlet Frances
Frances Bloom	Milligan Frances
Frances Etta Pearl	Dottie Frances
Frances Elle	Ree Frances
Frances Belle	Etta Frances
Frances Blair	Margot Frances Blue
Frances Wren	Adela Frances
Frances Ivy	Miller Frances

meaning

pronounced fran-siss | from France, or free one
English, France
#namesdailyfrances

Caro

Caro, besides that GORGEOUS meaning below, is also the Spanish word for expensive. So when you call your girl priceless?! Yes please. That "-o" ending?! Yes please. It's all the things that are sweet and powerful.

some pairing ideas

Caro Collins (Coco nickname, anyone???)
Caro Isabella
Caro Penelope
Caro Beatrix
Caro Elizabetta
Caro Bette
Caro Vess
Caro Violet
Caro Lucy
Caro Lucille

Eliza Caro
Junie Caro Dawn
Luna Caro
Julianna Caro
Reese Caro
Amelia Caro
Emmaline Caro
Luella Caro
Lucy Caro
India Caro

meaning

pronounced cair-row | dear, beloved
Italian, Portuguese
#namesdailycaro

Moore

The Scottish moors are dark, brooding, and romantic. Just scroll through some Scottish Instagrams and you'll be swooning in no time at all. It feels fearless and full of heart. And also, a lot of cool people have worn this as a last name. It's time it was moved to the front.

some pairing ideas

Moore Delilah	Ever Moore Like seriously, perfection.
Moore Winsley	Isla Moore
Moore Junie	Ella Winsley Moore
Moore Leslie	Della Moore
Moore Linden	Winona Moore
Moore Larkin	Tessa Moore
Moore Margaret	Marian Moore
Moore Tindra	Rilla Moore
Moore Louisa	Selena Moore
Moore Minoux	Etta Moore

meaning

pronounced more | one who lives by a moor | dark-skinned
English, Scottish, French
#namesdailymoore

Remi

It feels a little unisex without feeling vague. It's cute, poetic, and also feels a little Fast & Furious. If you're an outdoor/boating family, this is a living nod to that. This name feels so full of personality.

some pairing ideas

Remi Monroe	Willow Remi
Remi Dakota	Scout Remi
Remi Georgia	Noah Remi
Remi Alexandra	Adelaide Remi
Remi Zosia	Grace Remi
Remi Indigo	Antonia Remi
Remi Blue	Mattia Remi
Remi Violet	Elliott Remi
Remi True	Belle Remi
Remi Wynne	Roza Nelle Remi

meaning

pronounced remmy | oarsman
French, Latin
#namesdailyremi

58

Helena

Used by Shakespeare, Helena has beauty and moxie. She's also been an empress, queens, royalty, writers, activists, and other amazing women, which is no surprise because she's everything classy and deliberate.

some pairing ideas

Helena Dorothy	Scarlet Helena
Helena Charlotte	River Helena
Helena Marigold	Lucy Helena
Helena Jewel	Haddie Helena
Helena Whimsy	Rosie Helena
Helena Noelle	Lottie Helena
Helena Eve	Vesper Helena
Helena Sparrow	Maggie Helena
Helena Kate	Timber Helena
Helena Monroe	Ember Helena

meaning

pronounced huh-lay-nuh | bright, shining light | torch
Latin, Greek
#namesdailyhelena

Guide #name mentor

This is the "peacefully crafting your baby's name" part.

All the experiences my soul has been sifted through have brought me right here.

You'd think it would just be easy to name our child what our heart desires, but there seems to be a daunting headwind a lot of women face of all the "shouldn'ts" and "can'ts" spoken over us by other people.

I've heard a cry among women. I've seen firsthand the injustices done to not only their heart but their self-esteem. People's good intentions, as well as selfish intentions if I'm being honest, can equally make us doubt whether we know how to make right decisions. This is a hug rally and a reminder that you know what you're doing, and you need to elevate your own opinion. "You don't need to please everyone"... we hear this often. But do you believe it? All you will be responsible for at the end of the day is what you wrap your arms around. Everybody has to saddle up their own ponies.

I hope this guide, and this whole book really, gives you a space to think. I hope that when you turn the last page, you feel more clarity... that I can empower you to walk your own wishes and convictions. Do we recognize this baby will have his or her own identity, and life, and thoughts, etc? Yeah of course. Let's also recognize we get this incredible gift of carrying them in a way no one else will or can. Whether it's in utero, or through adoption, we help bring their story to life. It starts with them seeing you strong and at peace.

When we're wanting to step out in something, we're challenged with the people we place our value system in. When our loved ones, friends, or peers reject something, we take our personal conviction of stepping out in it as certain personal rejection. And let's be honest, it can be hard to stand inside a circle where no one else shares your opinion... and that's okay. The tragedy is when you sacrifice that place inside of you and let other people be the living filter of your decisions.

The first step to living an empowered life is recognizing you have power.

And don't think for a second that your soul in this finding-a-name journey has to sit at a conference table.

HOW TO NAME SAID BABY

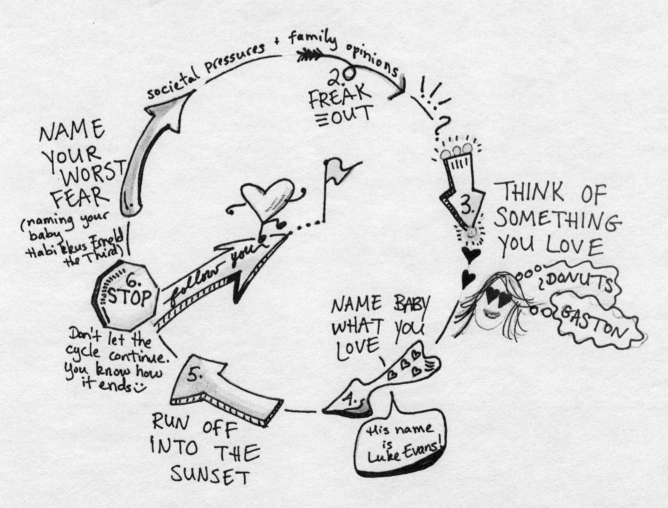

how to build a name

It can feel like a lot, this idea that we can control someone's first impression for a long time. Somebody had to chisel out Twrgadarn on a tombstone somewhere. You're like, "I love this name, but do I *love* this name? Will I hate it after the first family reunion? Will they hate it, and why does my partner seem to say no to everything? Am I allowed to quit and just call the baby Shnookums?"

Let me start off by saying... you've got this (insert strong arm emoji.) Like, totally for real, you do.

I think what happens is we easily get overwhelmed because we're trying to sift and filter too many things at once. There are one thousand hundred million decisions with this whole having a baby thing; am I right? Your baby will get a name.

"A person's name is to that person the sweetest, most important sound in any language."

I can't remember if that's Dale Carnegie's quote or that one time Scott Eastwood was reading to me in my dream, but it's true. So it's got to come from the heart if it's going to be said for one thousand hundred million times. And by "heart" I mean *your* heart, not Monnie-Tone from Target asking if you want the Red card.

Grab a pen and write all over this thing. Circle, highlight, scratch out. Do what makes you happy. Just don't use this as a fly swatter, k?

Find qualities instead of preferences. It's a more enjoyable road to travel down.

To the right, some quick thoughts for you on how to navigate the process.

one free range it

Hey, even organic sugar has to go through a process. Throw it out there... how does it make you feel to say it to someone you don't know, like a barista, or to a friend? Write your names on a Christmas card. Say it, sing it, throw it around like confetti.

If you put a new chicken out with an established flock, does it mesh well? Will it get pecked? Do you think it can grow cruelty-free? And remember, you're the head hen in your house. *xo*

two speak life over it

Names are people. Even the ones you don't like. I think sometimes we get fixated and forget to breathe our way through these decisions. Don't say a hard no, and make sure your partner doesn't either. Find ways to value each other's opinion, including your own. Don't sweat the small stuff, yet don't compromise the end goal, which is finding a name that makes you smile.

three endear it

Oh man. Opinionated opinions are hard to navigate. We value the opinions of those close to us so much, and I believe sometimes too much. ALWAYS follow your heart. You've already weighed everything, but don't get defeated if your favorite name isn't popular among your peeps. And there's a difference between someone in your corner caring for you and unsolicited advice. The difference? How do they make you feel, empowered or manipulated?

If you love it, keep it close to your heart and protect it. And also, saying "this is the name" comes across way different than "we're thinking of this name..."

You will be your sweetheart's greatest defender and cheerleader. Your heart knows the baby wants a donut, and trust your gut even with the name.

first names first

So you either have a list of names already or absolutely nothing but heartburn.

If you're having trouble getting bae involved in the process, here's a great way to intrigue him/her back in: instead of your separate preferences and "I dated someone with that name" and the "no way's," talk about the end game. What qualities are you looking for? How do you want your child to come across? I know you have some feelings about this. Talk about what you visualize.

When your little sweetheart tells your gasped secret in front of everyone, what name comes to mind that fills your heart with fondness?

If you don't have any definitive middle name(s), then my suggestion is to fall in love with the first name first. Get excited about this quest, or Quest Nathaniel. Don't get too tired or too discouraged to discover who this adorably poopy human is.

And to put your mind at ease, the hope is forever, but people change. Mark Twain was Samuel Clemens, John Wayne was Marion Morrison, Marilyn Monroe was Norma Jean, and Portia de Rossi was born Amanda Rogers. This name you're freaking out about is not a life sentence, just 18 years to life.

Some questions to talk about:

How does it sound with the last name. Do you like alliteration?

Does it make any weird initials?

Is it the same name of a societal or familial pain poin, i.e. Aunt Haggis, Decaf, Tuna?

Can you yell it with an arm full of groceries and shut the door with your foot?

Is it pleasant to spell and easy to understand? (I'm talking to you, Quinoa.)

Would you want to be named it or marry someone with that name? (Snuggling with a Crevice or Python or Hollygraph could be real buzzkill.)

meet in the middle

Maybe you know exactly what the middle name is going to be. Congratulations, job over. Or those two names you and your bae like but can't decide? Use them both!

Or maybe you're stuck. You really want something like The Edge (oh, can't you see what love has done?). I just love the middle name that takes you by surprise. It's FUN, peeps. Dance a jig, because the possibilities are endless. Just not Endless, okay?

Look right to see some of my personal favorites for inspiration. >>>>>>>>>

Some questions to talk about:

Do you want to honor someone, and are you sure you want it in the middle?

Are you a classic James/Lee/Rose/John/Ann/Jane/Mildred/Daniel/Folgers kinda person? Then just keep it simple.

Do you want them to be cool but not strange? Try nature names, like Aspen, River, or Moore. Places? London, Laramie, Canyon. Words like Poet, Ranger, Hawkeye, Scarlet (but no on Deets).

What are some of your favorite things, places? What moves you? Start there.

What speaks to you could very well be the beauty you call them into.

Jasper Everett Jude
Fox Hawk Bear
Landon Oakley Miles
Clive Radley Sparrow
Arrow Daisy Wren
Juniper Wynne Nelle
Tess Maisie Echo
Magnolia Golden
Odessa Adaline.

the seat of honor

Names on a global scale...

Should we be using names that aren't from our own personal heritage? For example, I think Aztec is a rad name. I think of the pattern, of course, because who doesn't. But, it's an origin, not a pattern, so there's the sticky wicket. Is it off limits or nah?

I think for me, I want to honor people. I want to give them the courtesy of something that speaks of them. In a small example, I would be hurt if someone who knew my grandfather used his name before me, because, common courtesy. Am I blessed they love him? Heck yeah! But it's in my territory and it's fastened into my life story and heart strings. You feel me?

These are just my thoughts, and I can't speak for you, unless you're going to order your coffee wrong at Starbucks. I'm leaving this here for you to consider.

Also... DUN DUN DUUUUUUNNNNNN

Name theft. It's real. Don't be a thiever unless it's essential oils.

And don't show everyone what's in the secret places of your heart unless you want them tracking mud everywhere. Hide yer kids, hide yer wife, etc.

A love note from me...

I know some of my encouragements are heavy, and you're probably already feeling information overload. If we were out having a coffee together, I would want you to feel relaxed. You have enough pressure. If I'm reaching out and touching something painful in your heart, it's because I want you to see you have a valve where you don't need to hold this all in. You can let go of people's expectations of you. I know you have the best of intentions. You take care of things. You love. You have kindness. You are worthy of being honored and respected. You got this.

honoring essence

Honoring...

Often we find ourselves in the place of wanting to honor somebody with a name that feels mismatched to a new person. A lot like an "outdated" appliance in a new kitchen. Does it fit? What's its charm?

I think we can get hung up on using it as is. It's okay to say "This is amazing for someone I love who is from a different time."

If honoring someone is on your heart, you aren't bound to their name. Names are fashion... you can honor blue jeans and not have to wear flares if you want skinny.

That's where, I believe, you draw in that person's essence.

Ask yourself this question to stretch you a little: if you weren't able to use their name (let's say they never had one), how would you honor them? Their scent when you hug them, their hobbies, their love language, their place of birth, their favorite song, color, flower, etc.

When you begin to unpack the things you love about someone, it starts to get really fun and re-energized.

"Dear old world," she murmured, "you are very lovely, and I am glad to be alive in you."
— Anne of Green Gables

when it comes down to it

Concerning the meaning of names...

When I hear people discarding a name because of its literal meaning, I start to pant. It's super unfortunate, because meaning is so relative and personal to you, and I want to prove my point out to you...

Milligan. It's a super cute and fun name, right?! But the meaning is "descendant of the bald-headed" and "to be tonsured." *slowly backs away*

The name Milligan in its original form dates back to 1207, when a man was ordained into being a monk in what is now known as Donegal, Ireland. From there, people took on this name, and years and years later anglicized it — some even changing it to Baldwin. Monks and individuals in other spiritual traditions across many religions, shaved the crown of their head as a sign of humility and purification. If you break down what tonsured means, it's the same as a sheep being shorn.

Being a farm girl, I now see this meaning in a more beautiful way. Have you ever seen an unshorn sheep? It's a painful and debilitating way for them to live.

So maybe, we could interpret the meaning as "a letting go." Maybe Milligan is a symbol of finding peace and cutting away what's not meant for you to carry. *mic drop* (Am I cool enough for that?)

So, when you see a name meaning, good or bad, see it as an opportunity to let it grow into full maturity. A name's meaning ultimately becomes what a person is. All of us have the opportunity to create a life that makes people feel happy when they say our name. If friends were flowers, right?

Maybe we should take meanings with a grain of salt, and a spoonful of sugar, and take back our power to be a people who conquer negativity and create magnificent things.

a well-worn path or a rut?

Alliteration...

Nine times out of ten, when I mention a name that starts with the same letter as someone's last name, they tell me they don't want that because it sounds like a superhero name. And then I ask them, "What's wrong with having a superhero name?" and then, nine times out of ten, they are caught off guard.

Does the first "no" reaction to things come because it actually bothers you, or because it's what you've always heard, or it's just a habit?

I don't know one boy who wouldn't want a superhero name. *(I hear that one person telling me her son doesn't like them right now lol.)* I think they are rad. It's totally fine if alliteration isn't your thing. But reconsider it.

Popularity...

You may have noticed, I didn't put the statistical ranking with my names. If you didn't know, the government collects all the names that have been used for babies each year and compiles that list. It's fun. Names are fashion, and it's an amazing thing to see what society was into that year. If you do know about it, and you've been there, you may have also noticed I have a few names in here that would be considered "popular," meaning, a lot of babies now wear that name.

The thing is, I just don't really want to focus on that. So many people have sacrificed their favorite name because of a number.

Years ago, basically everyone was named John. Then people had to create a second name to tell them apart... John the Smith... and then, last names were born. People have a way of creating beautiful things, and many coming together with a commonality isn't terrible because each one of them is their own person to begin with.

Traditions...

They're awesome until they're not. A heritage of character is way cooler.

"Never throughout history has a man who lived a life of ease left a name worth remembering."
— Theodore Roosevelt

meet the name mentor

Coffee sipper.
Kindness preacher.
Uneven hoodie strings fixer.
Instagram's 1st namer.

I've been immersed in the naming community for almost ten years. Interfacing with people, sharing moments and milestones in their lives, well, it's humbling, inspiring, and it's led me to experience a whole lot of naming. Look, I named my own little guy, so I know it is as serious as standstill traffic with a hungry pregnant woman with a full bladder.

/thenamementor   @namesdaily
thenamementor.com

cool story bro

Raising a son to be kind as he is brave, as respectful as he is fearless, as heroic as he is human, is a sacred thing. It's a privilege, and when I see my own about to skydive off the couch, it can be a terrifying thing. But it's also a beautiful, heart-deep journey. I want my son's name to be synonymous with all of the above qualities.

"It is a truth universally acknowledged that a single dude in possession of a good fortune must be because he's got a mad dope name." - *Jane Austen, Named and Prejudice*

We all know the heart is a well. And at the bottom of that well we have hammered and chiseled and guarded that hope for a beautiful world for our daughters. A world that's a garden and full of love, respect, and the dearness of humanness.

This begins with our sons.

I have one, and his heart is bursting with the wild ways of a man. It's beautiful and rugged. His being wants to scale the highest mountain and build the coolest gadget and roar with the bravest lion. And he also is wonderfully human. His heart is just as tender as my own feminine one because hearts are the same. They still feel so deeply, want to be affirmed, don't want to be called lesser, and the only danger is its getting broken.

These fifty boy names are wild and wonderful, creative and strong and fun. All of the qualities that make life an adventure, spanning time, ready for restless boys to embark on journeys that carry them into being wistful old men with enchanting life stories.

Congratulations on your boy!

— Alix, the name mentor

Silas

The name Silas is total dude package. Strong, manly, and yet holds the door open for you and brings you coffee. It feels wild and yet huggable. A rock climber, trail blazer, and fire stoker. Soft spoken, but holds his own.

some pairing ideas

Silas Fletcher	Henry Silas
Silas Fox	Holden Silas
Silas Everett	Philip Silas
Silas Oliver	Jude Silas
Silas Jameson	Remy Silas
Silas Holden	Oren Silas
Silas Champion	Robin Silas
Silas Rex	Weston Silas
Silas Orion	Corbin Silas
Silas True	Jett Silas

meaning

pronounced sigh-liss | man of the woods, or man of the forest
English from Latin
#namesdailysilas

Cove

Shelter. Safety. Quiet. The sea. The woods.
It is written in poetry and literature
and is basically a hipster dream.

some pairing ideas

Cove Jeremiah	Wesley Cove
Cove Nolan	Arthur Cove
Cove Gideon	Dashiell Cove
Cove Jasper	Ames Cove
Cove Malachy	Rory Cove
Cove Declan	Finley Cove
Cove Sterling	Linus Cove
Cove Dashiell	Emmett Cove
Cove Leland	Paxton Cove
Cove Westley	Niall Cove

meaning

pronounced kohv | a sheltered nook
Old English
#namesdailycove

Callum

It feels like Braveheart, and yet gentle at the same time.
Straight-forward with an air of mystery still.
Consummate light keeper, stargazer, and torch bringer.

some pairing ideas

Callum Desmond	Fox Callum
Callum Orion	Briar Callum
Callum Frost	Niles Callum
Callum Bravery	Ridge Callum
Callum Brave	Radley Callum
Callum True	Roe Callum
Callum Jesse	Rory Callum
Callum Wilder	Rafe Callum
Callum Sterling	Denver Callum
Callum Fletcher	Arthur Callum

meaning

pronounced cal-lum | dove
Scottish
#namesdailycallum

74

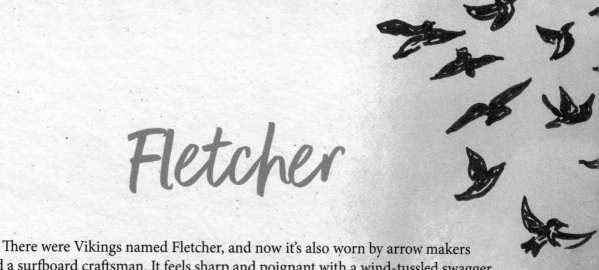

Fletcher

There were Vikings named Fletcher, and now it's also worn by arrow makers and a surfboard craftsman. It feels sharp and poignant with a wind-tussled swagger and probably knows how to make a good coconut milk latte.

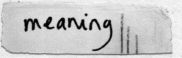

some pairing ideas

Fletcher Fox	Sterling Fletcher
Fletcher Ingram	Callum Fletcher
Fletcher Henry	Bodhi Fletcher
Fletcher Nahum	Koa Fletcher
Fletcher Jack	Thomas Fletcher
Fletcher Leland	Leland Fletcher
Fletcher Aspen	Kai Fletcher
Fletcher Moses	Calvin Fletcher
Fletcher Jude	Ruskin Fletcher
Fletcher Sterling	Hollis Fletcher

meaning

pronounced flet-cher | maker of arrows | people's army
Old English

#namesdailyfletcher

Finch

Finch is winsome with a southern soul cry. Colorful with earth tones, friendly and playful. Yet it holds a serious side that takes it from preschool to major. Want to see a beautiful sight? Goldfinches in the winter.

some pairing ideas

Finch Everett	Callum Finch
Finch Declan	Cleo Finch
Finch Aaron	Crosby Finch
Finch Ames	Jack Finch
Finch Burton	Judah Finch
Finch Tennyson	Rafferty Finch
Finch Arthur	Matthew Finch
Finch Brighton	Walter Finch
Finch Everest	Howie Finch
Finch Holden	Koa Finch

meaning

pronounced finch | a songbird
Old English
#namesdailyfinch

Crosby

Crosby feels creative and edgy in a way that still feels tied to classic roots.
When I think of Crosby I think of sweet tea, a colorful sunrise, the ocean.
It makes me think of a good book and a sweet letter and vibrant colors.

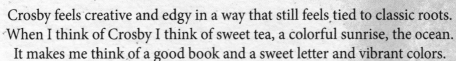

some pairing ideas

Crosby Isaiah	Val Crosby
Crosby Jonah	Emmett Crosby
Crosby Jem	Saxo Crosby
Crosby Desmond	Indiana Crosby
Crosby Emmett	Ewan Crosby
Crosby Jordan	Gideon Crosby
Crosby Truett	Paxton Crosby
Crosby Farrow	Nolan Crosby
Crosby River	Asher Crosby
Crosby Oak	Cooper Crosby

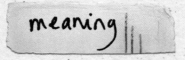

meaning

pronounced crawz-bee | village of crosses
Irish
#namesdailycrosby

Ames

Take away the "J" in James and you're left with something pointed in a cool direction. A little hipster, a little old world. I can see it on a cowboy as well as a president. A cool fact: Ames is also a NASA Research Center. Ames can count his lucky stars.

some pairing ideas

Ames Oliver	Weston Ames
Ames Casper	Cecil Ames
Ames Wilder	Dashiell Ames
Ames Tennyson	Wesley Ames
Ames Everest	Jude Ames
Ames Jacoby	Gareth Ames
Ames Filipe	Bear Ames
Ames Jasper	Topher Ames
Ames Noel	Benjamin Ames
Ames Oakley	Nicolas Ames

meaning

pronounced aims | friend, beloved
French
#namesdailyames

Fox

Playful. Woodsy. A Swifty probably. Or do I mean swift?
Definitely listens to indie folk music and avoids chain coffee companies
and loves flannel. And cute. And very smoochable.

some pairing ideas

Fox Leland	Winston Fox
Fox Everett	Desmond Fox
Fox Wyatt	Evren Fox
Fox Easton	Cairo Fox
Fox Charlie	Ronan Fox
Fox Declan	Callum Fox
Fox Neo	Burton Fox
Fox Aaron	Jorian Fox
Fox Devlin	Milo Fox
Fox Benedict	Holden Fox

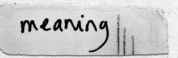

meaning

pronounced focks | thick-haired tail
to be cunning or crafty
German, English
#namesdailyfox

Arrow

Longfellow wrote it into timelessness. "The Arrow and the Song."
Words and actions can be so pointed with kindness and determination
and friendship, and love always hits its mark. I can't think of a
sweeter depiction for Arrow than that.

some pairing ideas

Arrow Philip	Dorian Arrow
Arrow Titus	Declan Arrow
Arrow Sterling	Rafe Arrow
Arrow Finley	Ronan Arrow
Arrow Henry	Vaughn Arrow
Arrow Miguel	Quinn Arrow
Arrow Arthur	Pax Arrow
Arrow Calloway	Daxton Arrow
Arrow Jenks	Macsen Arrow
Arrow Judah	Jude Arrow

meaning

pronounced air-row | belonging to the bow
German
#namesdailyarrow

Ruskin

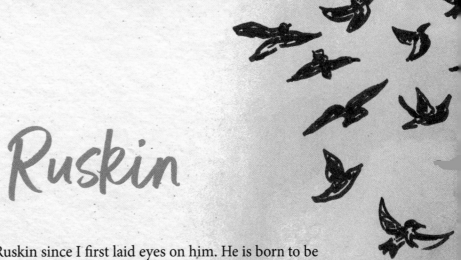

I've loved the name Ruskin since I first laid eyes on him. He is born to be the hero in a story that gets passed down in awed tones, no? I think of corn husks and the brilliant colors of autumn, and grit, and wonder, and the glorious toned filter that hangs over everything Scotland.

some pairing ideas

Ruskin Milo	Callum Ruskin
Ruskin Wilder	Wyatt Ruskin
Ruskin Farrow	Jude Ruskin
Ruskin James	Ollie Ruskin
Ruskin Armor	Ethan Ruskin
Ruskin Arthur	Caleb Ruskin
Ruskin Alastair	Cody Ruskin
Ruskin Hamish	Emmett Ruskin
Ruskin True	Clyde Ruskin
Ruskin Wallace	Samuel Ruskin

meaning

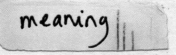

pronounced russ-kin | from a family of tanners | little nose
Scottish, German
#namesdailyruskin

Dashiell

Dash was made for Christmastime. It's an evergreen name that is darling on a baby but legit for a grown man. Can you imagine a Grampa Dash?! Or a guy named Dash who looks an awful lot like Clark Kent? Dash meets Ansel Elgort. I just threw a lot of visuals at you, sorry. It's just a name that's Incredible.

some pairing ideas

Dashiell River	Jory Dashiell
Dashiell Gaspard	Sterling Dashiell
Dashiell Thomas	Colton Dashiell
Dashiell Pierre	Fox Dashiell
Dashiell Avery	Julien Dashiell
Dashiell Mercer	Clive Dashiell
Dashiell Saint	Aubin Dashiell
Dashiell Grey	Blaze Dashiell
Dashiell Pépin	Luc Dashiell
Dashiell True	Reeve Dashiell

meaning

pronounced dash-uhl | page boy or young man
French
#namesdailydashiell

Arlo

This name loves allegory and story. It creates an image of old world and time tested, but also philosophically folky and fun.

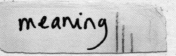
some pairing ideas

Arlo Hemingway	Paxton Arlo
Arlo Frost	John Arlo
Arlo Grant	Fox Arlo
Arlo Montgomery	Desi Arlo
Arlo Reggie	Frost Arlo
Arlo Burton	Jameson Arlo
Arlo Clancy	Winter Arlo
Arlo Juniper	Sage Arlo
Arlo Gregor	Calvin Arlo
Arlo Finch	Cade Arlo

meaning

pronounced ar-low | bayberry tree | fortified hill
Spanish, German
#namesdailyarlo

Clancy

A man who can depict thrilling strength and draws out talented men.
He's also ridden along the banks of Snowy River as an Australian cowboy.
Its sound is a bit musical, fun, and feels like it can always bring 'round the cheer.

some pairing ideas

Clancy Oak	Robin Clancy
Clancy Everest	Scout Clancy
Clancy Ridge	Rowan Clancy
Clancy Sky	August Clancy
Clancy Denver	Otis Clancy
Clancy Malone	Theo Clancy
Clancy Beau	Titan Clancy
Clancy Frost	Howard Clancy
Clancy Jack	Leonard Clancy
Clancy Roe	Benjamin Clancy

meaning

pronounced clan-see | red-haired warrior
Irish
#namesdailyclancy

Leland

If there was a modern adaption of King Arthur, I can see Leland as a knight seated at the round table.

some pairing ideas

Leland Shiloh	True Leland
Leland Noah	Davis Leland
Leland Parker	Shay Leland
Leland Orion	Isaiah Leland
Leland Fletcher	Noah Leland
Leland Scout	Merit Leland
Leland Josiah	Otto Leland
Leland True	West Leland
Leland Zephyr	Blake Leland
Leland Sparrow	Koda Leland

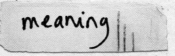

meaning

pronounced lee-lind | meadow land or pasture ground
English

#namesdailyleland

Robin

Robin is a name that, despite becoming famous with his teddy bear, was cultured, like its beautiful minty blue eggs, in the female spectrum. But robins aren't afraid to be bold with their orange-flagged bellies and be the BFF of Batman. Robin is rugged and and handsome and definitely ready to fly away home to the boy's nest.

some pairing ideas

note:
*And also, to give credit to my boy-love for this, it fell out of the Top 1,000 names for girls in 2004 and only popped back in at #974 in 2018. Aaaaaand, coincidentally, it has been spotted back on the boys' list. #yasssss

Robin Luke	Radley Robin
Robin Patrick	Ames Robin
Robin Arthur	Sterling Robin
Robin Gallagher	Theo Robin
Robin Matteo	Sawyer Robin
Robin Emmett	Hollis Robin
Robin Josiah	Bennett Robin
Robin Gerard	Bodhi Robin
Robin Radley	Hugh Robin
Robin Davy	Aleks Robin

meaning

pronounced rob-bin | bright, shining fame | a bird
German, English from Old French
#namesdailyrobin

Calder

First spoken in a Scottish brogue and feels like it's meant to be sung in the highlands.
Or in a nursery. Or hollered out the front door that you're so glad he's home.
Calder feels like home, but the kind of home you say "when I'm with you."

some pairing ideas

Calder Isaiah	William Calder
Calder Truet	Truett Calder
Calder Hollis	Andrew Calder
Calder Oak	Jem Calder
Calder Emmett	John Calder
Calder Winsome	Everett Calder
Calder Beckham	Livingston Calder
Calder Boone	Ames Calder
Calder Jem	Wyatt Calder
Calder Avery	Oakley Calder

meaning

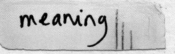

pronounced call-der | from the wild water, or the woods between waters
Scottish
#namesdailycalder

Sterling

A strong man who stays true to himself and his personal convictions.
I see Sterling as a kind, brave, resolute protector.

some pairing ideas

Sterling Winslow	Asher Sterling
Sterling Arlo	Lionel Sterling
Sterling Woodrow	Calvin Sterling
Sterling Jacob	Callum Sterling
Sterling Lewis	Jem Sterling
Sterling Asher	Ronan Sterling
Sterling Grady	Nehemiah Sterling
Sterling Oakley	Orion Sterling
Sterling Wesley	Matthew Sterling
Sterling Alby	Creed Sterling

meaning

pronounced stur-ling | thoroughly excellent
of the highest quality
English
#namesdailysterling

Finley

It is true: I am in love with this name. I've loved it, in fact, since I was a really young girl. It made such a positive and happy impression on me that it still makes me happy. It's as lush and scenic as any Irish heritage and feels as cozy as a fire on a rainy day. And the nickname Finn... #love

some pairing ideas

Finley Brighton	Calder Finley
Finley Brave	Arthur Finley
Finley Wilder	Wes Finley
Finley Burton	River Finley
Finley Andrew	Kellin Finley
Finley Gallagher	Langston Finley
Finley Macsen	Truett Finley
Finley Reuben	Ronan Finley
Finley Evergreen	Clarence Finley
Finley Micah	Arlo Finley

meaning

pronounced fin-lee | fair-headed warrior
Irish
#namesdailyfinley

Calvin

He's not just a cute kid with a Tiger friend. He also knows all about style. Cal, seriously, is like the coolest nickname. (Besides all of the other nicknames I say are the coolest.) Calvin is both handsome and playful, and I love it.

some pairing ideas

Calvin Jude	Arthur Calvin
Calvin Gregor	Miles Calvin
Calvin Juno	Leo Calvin
Calvin Milo	Wesley Calvin
Calvin Saxo	Henry Calvin
Calvin Jem	Theo Calvin
Calvin Phillip	Bo Calvin
Calvin Grady	Bear Calvin
Calvin Brady	Finley Calvin
Calvin West	Moe Calvin

meaning

pronounced cal-vin | bald, hairless refer to page 58 about meanings

Latin

#namesdailycalvin

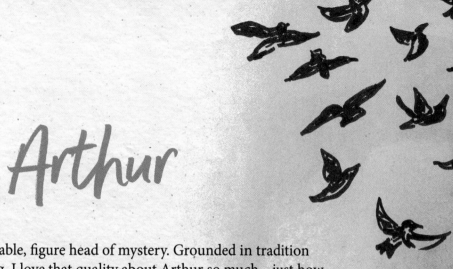

Arthur

Head of the round table, figure head of mystery. Grounded in tradition and folklore. It's strong. I love that quality about Arthur so much—just how strong it is. It never gets tired. Truly a name for generations.

some pairing ideas

Arthur Van	Wes Arthur
Arthur Finn	Owen Arthur
Arthur Seacliff	Orion Arthur
Arthur Quimby	Cruz Arthur
Arthur Maxwell	Nole Arthur
Arthur Nahum	Oak Arthur
Arthur Beck	Oakley Arthur
Arthur Bentley	Reid Arthur
Arthur Declan	Reeve Arthur
Arthur Bow	Jem Arthur

meaning

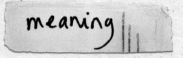

pronounced ar-thir | noble, courageous or bear-like
English
#namesdailyarthur

Koa

Koa has every quality to be as popular as Noah...but he isn't popular at all!
Another neat thing is that he is the Hawaiian word for
acacia tree which is used for surfboards. How cool is that?!

some pairing ideas

Koa Fletcher	Archer Koa
Koa Radley	Christian Koa
Koa Wilder	Bennett Koa
Koa Wilds	Topher Koa
Koa Evander	River Koa
Koa Nolan	Chase Koa
Koa Blake	Indy Koa
Koa Macsen	Rafferty Koa
Koa Everett True	Sloane Koa
Koa River	Bear Koa

meaning

pronounced koh-uh | brave | acacia tree
Hawaiian
#namesdailykoa

Ronan

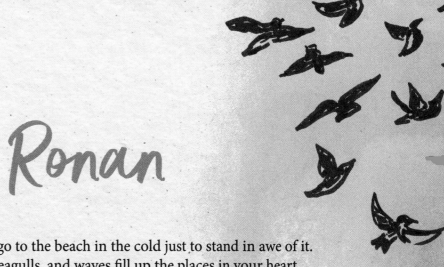

Those days when you go to the beach in the cold just to stand in awe of it.
Long shadows and seagulls, and waves fill up the places in your heart.
"I remember your bare feet down the hallway.
I love you to the moon and back." - *Taylor Swift*

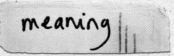

Ronan Beckett	August Ronan
Ronan Ames	Silas Ronan
Ronan Wilder	Fox Ronan
Ronan Brave	Jet Ronan
Ronan James	Miles Ronan
Ronan Grady	Lark Ronan
Ronan Juniper	Rex Ronan
Ronan Matthew	Navy Ronan
Ronan Jasper	Cal Ronan
Ronan August	Charles Ronan

meaning

pronounced row-nin | little seal
Irish
n a m e s d a i l y r o n a n

Burton

Solid in winter sports, and can hold his own on the silver screen.
There are many strong and creative Burton's, and I got to know one personally.
It's the comfort of your grandpa's sweater, and while there's the obvious
nickname Burt/Burtie, there's also Bo, and, uh, Guster.

some pairing ideas →

Burton Everest	Chevy Burton
Burton Calloway	Davy Burton
Burton Hadley	Koa Burton
Burton Iver (please let me)	Stanley Burton
Burton Holiday	Howie Burton
Burton Maverick	Clarence Burton
Burton Leo	Rex Burton
Burton Jasper	Finley Burton
Burton Winter	Ford Burton
Burton Clive	Zac Burton

meaning

pronounced burr-tin | fortified enclosure, or fortified town
Old English
#namesdailyburton

Clarence

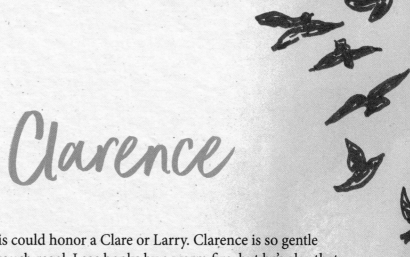

I love how this could honor a Clare or Larry. Clarence is so gentle yet so full and a touch regal. I see books by a warm fire, but he's also that friend you can always call on who visits with his grandma and is just a good, solid, witty, kind guy.

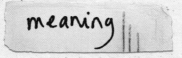

some pairing ideas

Clarence Jazz	Lev Clarence
Clarence Willoughby	Hawk Clarence
Clarence Ridgely	Wolf Clarence
Clarence Ember	Briar Clarence
Clarence Deveraux	Rupert Clarence
Clarence River	Reuben Clarence
Clarence Fox	Indigo Clarence
Clarence Montgomery	Wilder Clarence
Clarence Finch	Gray Clarence
Clarence North	Sasha Clarence

meaning

pronounced clair-ins | bright, illustrious
from Latin
#namesdailyclarence

Casper

I get tired of people only associating this name with the friendly ghost, and honestly, what's wrong with a friendly ghost? The name Casper is an extremely ancient name, and was even one of the Magi. This name has lived through much history, and is still as beautiful today.

some pairing ideas

Casper Jude	Leo Casper
Casper John	Drue Casper
Casper Viggo	Abel Casper
Casper Jonah	Hal Casper
Casper Finley	Angelo Casper
Casper Finn	Knight Casper
Casper Vallen	Badgely Casper
Casper Livingstone	Van Casper
Casper Ellwood	Bowie Casper
Casper Wyatt	Wyatt Casper

meaning

pronounced cass-per | treasurer | keeper of the treasure
Dutch, Persian
#namesdailycasper

Evren

It feels somewhere in the middle of Aaron and Evan.
It comes from Turkish mythology — the name of the "dragons"
that live in the mountains and in caves to protect the treasures.
It just has such a fun, cool vibe to it.

some pairing ideas

Evren Leo	Bo Evren
Evren Chase	Mac Evren
Evren Milo	Cruz Evren
Evren Miles	Axel Evren
Evren Theo	Ridge Evren
Evren Topher	Matthew Evren
Evren Mitchell	Kai Evren
Evren Stone	Bay Evren
Evren Sparrow	Rhys Evren
Evren Cole	Cole Evren

meaning

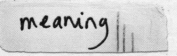

pronounced ev-rin | the heavens, the cosmos
Turkish
#namesdailyevren

Clive

If you're a fan of Arthurian legend, put Clive on your list.
Clive Owen brought Arthur to life in an amazing way (that movie
was unreal good). Poetry, music, the arts, writing, and sports
have all seen Clive. It has that classic gent vibe.

some pairing ideas

Clive Desmond	Aspen Clive
Clive Ingram	Inman Clive
Clive Arthur	Leon Clive
Clive Willoughby	William Clive
Clive Theodore	Teddy Clive
Clive Moses	Moe Clive
Clive Winston	Weston Clive
Clive James	Newton Clive
Clive Jameson	Jameson Clive
Clive Thomas	Thomas Clive

meaning

pronounced clive | cliff dweller
English
#namesdailyclive

Rafe

It feels very colonial, but actually has its roots on the other side of the pond.
It feels rugged, straight-forward, and handsome.
Could honor a Ralph (Waldo Emerson anyone???)

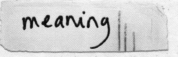

some pairing ideas

Rafe Emerson	Sterling Rafe
Rafe Milo	Delcan Rafe
Rafe Wilder	Finley Rafe
Rafe Lawrence	Miles Rafe
Rafe Indigo	Blue Rafe
Rafe Augustine	Callum Rafe
Rafe Indiana	Inman Rafe
Rafe Atticus	Tennyson Rafe
Rafe Leopold	Benjamin Rafe
Rafe Wyatt	Wyatt Rafe

meaning

pronounced raif | wolf counsel, or wise wolf
Old Norse
#namesdailyrafe

Judah

A tribe, a place, a heritage, an army of music...
Judah is a strong name that lights up a room. It's possible
I'm thinking of my own son Judah, but it's still true.

some pairing ideas

Judah Landon	Davy Judah
Judah Rafferty	Radley Judah
Judah Brighton	Brighton Judah
Judah Cannon	Heath Judah
Judah Finch	Ember Judah
Judah Robin	Robin Judah
Judah Declan	Declan Judah
Judah Wilder	Crosby Judah
Judah Ruskin	Ruskin Judah
Judah Livingstone	Remy Judah

meaning

pronounced joo-duh | praised | to praise
Hebrew
#namesdailyjudah

Radley

Atticus and Scout are getting love but don't forget the under-celebrated Radley. Rad, the next gen of Brad, is a cool cat. It has a free sound and friendly cadence and definitely deserves to be considered.

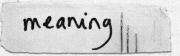
some pairing ideas

Radley Isaiah	Isaiah Radley
Radley Archer	Finn Radley
Radley Judah	Macsen Radley
Radley Hawk	Hawk Radley
Radley Tobin	Tobin Radley
Radley Golden	Valen Radley
Radley Emmett	Emmett Radley
Radley Theodore	Theo Radley
Radley Austin	Boone Radley
Radley Pierce	Hayes Radley

meaning

pronounced rad-lee | red meadow | from the red field
English
#namesdailyradley

Orion

Orion is not only a star in the sky but a star in cool factor.
It's a name that is thousands of years old, and yet is very low
in usage, making it shine with potential.
Did you know Mark Twain had a brother named Orion?

some pairing ideas

Orion Matthias	Henry Orion
Orion Matthew	Jude Orion
Orion Clarence	Clarence Orion
Orion Sterling	Sterling Orion
Orion Saxo	Wolf Orion
Orion Arthur	Archie Orion
Orion Maximus	Bear Orion
Orion Jory	Banks Orion
Orion Benedict	Rupert Orion
Orion Jasper	Hendrix Orion

meaning

pronounced or-eye-in | boundary, limit | the mighty hunter
Greek
#namesdailyorion

Saxo

A name that's medieval and ends with the "-o" sound is pretty rad in my book. (Wait, this is my book.) Saxo Grammaticus was a scholar and historian who first wrote about the history of Denmark. Can you even imagine introducing yourself as Saxo?!

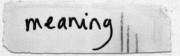

some pairing ideas

Saxo Lucas	Aksel Saxo
Saxo Victor	Arne Saxo
Saxo Knightley	Storm Saxo
Saxo Elias	Abel Saxo
Saxo Creed	Abram Saxo
Saxo Anakin	Leif Saxo
Saxo Adrian	Alvin Saxo
Saxo Elias	Berner Saxo
Saxo Gregor	Wolf Saxo
Saxo Nicholas/Niklas	Arthur Saxo

meaning

pronounced sax-oh | swordsman, or warrior
Old Norse
#namesdailysaxo

Everest

A mighty name indeed. Mt. Everest is Earth's highest mountain above sea level. People dream of it. In personal terms, someone's everest is the high point in their life, i.e. that day a child changed your life.

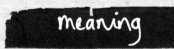

some pairing ideas

Everest Gilbert	Cam Everest
Everest Reuben	Reuben Everest
Everest Ames	Axel Everest
Everest Dashiell	Luther Everest
Everest Burton	Breckin Everest
Everest John	John Everest
Everest Brave	Bowie Everest
Everest Arlo	Arlo Everest
Everest Jack	Jack Everest
Everest Luke	Lou Everest

meaning

pronounced ev-uh-rist | highest mountain | high point, summit
strong as a wild boar, or Everett's son
German
#namesdailyeverest

Howard

I've loved this name for a seriously long time.
It's old-timey and fun and finger-snappin'.
And the nickname Howie, good day.

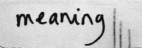
some pairing ideas

Howard Fox	Fox Howard
Howard Fletcher	Jem Howard
Howard Sterling	Silas Howard
Howard Hawk	Hawkins Howard
Howard Langston	Langston Howard
Howard Knox	Knox Howard
Howard Oakley	Oakley Howard
Howard Linus	Linus Howard
Howard Hollis	Rex Howard
Howard Miles	Miles Howard

meaning

pronounced how-werd | high guardian, or brave heart
Old English
#namesdailyhoward

True

Modern virtue? Sounds a little like Drew
and a lot like something really special.

True Everett	Callum True
True Crosby	Remy True
True Clancy	Atticus True
True Augustus	Lyle True
True Niall	Micah True
True Evander	Ollie True
True Blake	Oliver True
True Connolly	Finnigan True
True Gallagher	Misha True
True Vincent	Sasha True

meaning

pronounced trew | real, genuine, authentic, sincere
and not deceitful
English
#namesdailytrue

Alden

Alden dates back to the 11th century which maybe is why it feels like, just like its meaning says, an old friend.

some pairing ideas

Alden Wesley	Wes Alden
Alden Casper	Cam Alden
Alden Windsor	North Alden
Alden Beckett	Beck Alden
Alden Harvey	Harris Alden
Alden Fox	Fox Alden
Alden Wright	Jem Alden
Alden Beeker	Booker Alden
Alden George	William Alden
Alden Maverick	Destry Alden

meaning

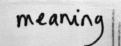

pronounced all-din | old friend
Old English
#namesdailyalden

Jem

L. M. Montgomery gifted the earth with this name: "Jem, of the steady lips and fearless eyes..." In her books, Jem was short for James, but it carries so well on its own. Also, Jem Finch, so what's not to love about this name?!

some pairing ideas

Jem Fletcher	Fletcher Jem
Jem Alexander	Evander Jem
Jem Rafferty	Rafferty Jem
Jem Theodore	Theo Jem
Jem Roosevelt	Koa Jem
Jem Finley	Finley Jem
Jem Winston	Reuben Jem
Jem Willoughby	Otis Jem
Jem Destry	Ridgeley Jem
Jem Rhys	Micah Jem

meaning

pronounced jem | supplanter
English
#namesdailyjem

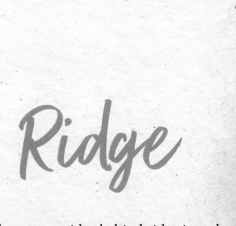

Ridge

"Eastward the dawn rose, ridge behind ridge into the morning,
and vanished out of eyesight into guess; it was no more than a
glimmer blending with the hem of the sky, but it spoke to them,
out of memory and old tales, of the high and distant mountains." - *Tolkien*

some pairing ideas

Ridge Benedict	Dashiell Ridge
Ridge Malachy	Macsen Ridge
Ridge Amadeus	Ames Ridge
Ridge Matthew	Matthew Ridge
Ridge Devlin	Dylan Ridge
Ridge Declan	Declan Ridge
Ridge Jacoby	Coby Ridge
Ridge Augustine	Alden Ridge
Ridge Truett	Truett Ridge
Ridge Lucas	Luke Ridge

meaning

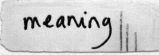

pronounced ridg | a chain of hills or mountains
the long and narrow upper edge or crest of something
English
#namesdailyridge

Wilder

"We need the tonic of wildness... At the same time that we are earnest to explore and learn all things, we require that all things be mysterious and unexplorable, that land and sea be indefinitely wild, unsurveyed and unfathomed by us because unfathomable. We can never have enough of nature." - *Henry David Thoreau*

some pairing ideas

Wilder Joshua	William Wilder
Wilder Christian	Banks Wilder
Wilder Truman	Teddy Wilder
Wilder Livingstone	Lennon Wilder
Wilder Emmett	Emmett Wilder
Wilder Ames	Ames Wilder
Wilder Finn	Finley Wilder
Wilder Knox	Bennett Wilder
Wilder Jude	Abe Wilder
Wilder Hollis	Van Wilder

meaning

pronounced while-der | hunter | wild and passionate
living wild and untamed in nature
English, German
#namesdailywilder

Winsome

A boy (and a man) with a winsome smile can be so
disarming. It feels friendly and like a book full of
poetry and adventure. Handsome, open, and a best friend.
Wim, Winny, and Wes could be fun nicknames.

some pairing ideas

Winsome Joe	Lyle Winsome
Winsome Cassidy	Carlo Winsome
Winsome Beck	John Winsome
Winsome Thomas	Theo Winsome James
Winsome Laurie	Todd Winsome James
Winsome Craig	Colton Winsome
Winsome Grey	Alex Winsome
Winsome Grady	Grady Winsome
Winsome Clyde	Clyde Winsome
Winsome Arlo	Arlo Winsome

meaning

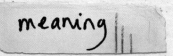

pronounced wyn-sum | joysome | charming; winning; engaging
Middle English
#namesdailywinsome

Van

Van feels so much like the son of John or Max. Grandpa might be all like "Like Van Halen?!" but thankfully this generation is all about finding adventire in schoolies and taking chances on dreams and Ed Sheeran/Ariana Grande. Van is freakin' cool... that's just me thinkin' out loud.

some pairing ideas

Van Everett	George Van
Van Everest	Leo Van
Van Rafferty	Rafferty Van
Van Deveraux	Devlin Van
Van Amadeus	Titus Van
Van Reginald	Reggie Van
Van Tobias	Toby Van
Van Titus	Hollis Van
Van Dashiell	Dorian Van
Van Sparrow	Saxo Van

meaning

pronounced van | type of old winnowing machine
of, from
French, English
#namesdailyvan

112

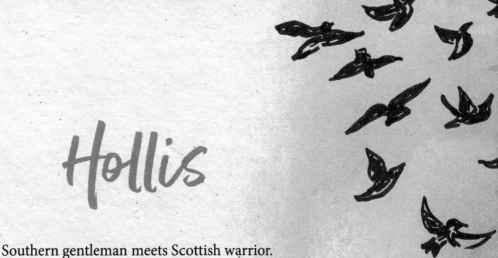

Hollis

Southern gentleman meets Scottish warrior.

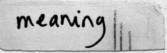
some pairing ideas

Hollis River	River Hollis
Hollis Graeme	Paxton Hollis
Hollis Brave	Birghton Hollis
Hollis Andrew	Anderson Hollis
Hollis Creighton	Corbin Hollis
Hollis Montgomery	Leon Hollis
Hollis Wilder	Boone Hollis
Hollis Tolkien	Bear Hollis
Hollis Westley	Remy Hollis
Hollis Wyatt	John Hollis

meaning

pronounced hahl-iss | dweller at the holly trees
Anglo-Saxon
#namesdailyhollis

Lyle

"Home is where my horse is." - *Lyle Lovett*
That's exactly how I picture the name Lyle.

some pairing ideas

Lyle Boomer	Holden Lyle
Lyle Henry	Mick Lyle
Lyle Jett	Corbin Lyle
Lyle Macsen	Benedict Lyle
Lyle Jacob	Van Lyle
Lyle Everest	Fenton Lyle
Lyle Robin	Gibson Lyle
Lyle Raven	Booker Lyle
Lyle Kenneth	Jameson Lyle
Lyle Finnick	Emmett Lyle

meaning

pronounced lile | island, or dweller of the isle
English, French
#namesdailylyle

114

Teddy

While I know Theo and Theodore are rad, Teddy comes
with such an endearment. And yes, I do see Teddy on a grown man,
and yes, I hope that man knows the importance of hugs and snuggles.

some pairing ideas

Teddy Winston	Winston Teddy
Teddy Lawrence	Linden Teddy
Teddy Macsen	Rafe Teddy
Teddy Knute	Bo Teddy
Teddy Seamus	Arlo Teddy
Teddy Reid	Cameron Teddy
Teddy Fenton	Joel Teddy
Teddy Radbourne	Rosen Teddy
Teddy Ruskin	Booker Teddy
Teddy Heathcliff	Oliver Teddy

meaning

pronounced teddy | gift of God | wealthy guardian
a soft toy bear
English
n a m e s d a i l y t e d d y

115

Sparrow

Sparrows crave connection. They protect where they live and sing.
In legend, they are the soul catchers. Sailors would engrave their skin
with sparrows so in case they were lost at sea, their soul could still find its way
home. This name feels like an old soul, doesn't it?

some pairing ideas

Sparrow Elijah	Easton Sparrow
Sparrow Glenn	George Sparrow
Sparrow Lucas	Lumi Sparrow
Sparrow Philip	Peyton Sparrow
Sparrow Judah	Grady Sparrow
Sparrow Landon	Kasen Sparrow
Sparrow Declan	Declan Sparrow
Sparrow James	Jory Sparrow
Sparrow Finley	Finley Sparrow
Sparrow John	John Sparrow

meaning

pronounced spair-row | small field bird, its root meaning speed
a homey, quick witted, lively person
Old English, Germanic
#namesdailysparrow

Linus

The sweetest name for a little peanut who can also
hold his own with the mythological Greeks through his sweet
musician skills. I pray people toss the blanket of doubt
and embrace Linus for the gem he is.

some pairing ideas

Linus Cole	Paxton Linus
Linus Matthew	Theodore Linus
Linus Fox	Rook Linus
Linus Theo	Toby Linus
Linus Evander	Ever Linus
Linus Arlo	Decker Linus
Linus Renn	Jordy Linus
Linus Phillip	Elvy Linus
Linus Gregor	Booker Linus
Linus Cobalt	Alby Linus

meaning

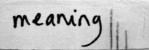

pronounced line-iss | flax
Greek
#namesdailylinus

Hawk + Hawke

Hawk/Hawke has wings, history, and stature.
"Anyone who has ever stopped to watch a hawk in flight will know that this is one of the natural world's most elegant phenomena." - *John Burnside*

some pairing ideas

Hawk Brighton	Samuel Hawke
Hawk Rafferty	Rafferty Hawke
Hawk Aaron	Aaron Hawk
Hawk Rafe	Burton Hawk
Hawke Arlo	Arthur Hawk
Hawke Maximus	Bridger Hawke
Hawk Evander	Grady Hawke
Hawk Leo	Finley Hawk
Hawk Tennyson	Miles Hawk
Hawk Inman	Tannen Hawke

meaning

pronounced hawk | hawk, hawker
Anglo-Saxon
#namesdailyhawk   #namesdailyhawke

Langston

Filled with as much honor as Booker and Angelou. What can I say? #goals
"Hold fast to dreams, for if dreams die, life is a broken-winged bird that cannot fly."
"My soul has grown deep like the rivers."
- *Langston Hughes*

some pairing ideas

Langston Oak	Harvey Langston
Langston Miles	Miles Langston
Langston True	Walter Langston
Langston Sparrow	Sparrow Langston
Langston Wilder	Rhys Langston
Langston Chord	Chord Langston
Langston Milo	Ember Langston
Langston Arthur	Arne Langston
Langston River	River Langston
Langston Clive	Cleo Langston

meaning

pronounced lang-stin | tall man's town, or long stone
Old English
#namesdailylangston

Tennyson

If you tell me poetry isn't cool, then I will show you Russell Crowe
and I'll cash you outside, how bout dat! Lolz all kidding aside,
Tennyson is both poetic and manly and Tenny is a fun nickname.
"My strength is as the strength of ten, because my heart is pure." - *Lord Tennyson*

some pairing ideas

Tennyson Fox	Fox Tennyson
Tennyson Hawk	Arlo Tennyson
Tennyson Judah	Rudy Tennyson
Tennyson Jude	Saxo Tennyson
Tennyson Gregor	Gray Tennyson
Tennyson Carlo	Lando Tennyson
Tennyson Arthur	Arthur Tennyson
Tennyson Matthew	Matthew Tennyson
Tennyson Philip	Phlip Tennyson
Tennyson Blake	Blakely Tennyson

meaning

pronounced ten-uh-sin | son of Dennis
or you could say, the son of the son of Dionysius
English
#namesdailytennyson

120

Rudy

I always picture Rudy as fun and quick-witted, someone you want on your team. And the nickname Roo makes this name even more lovable.

some pairing ideas

Rudy Winston	Winston Rudy
Rudy Fisher	Atlas Rudy
Rudy Wilder	Albion Rudy
Rudy Banks	Wes Rudy
Rudy Hollis	Hollis Rudy
Rudy Miles	Milo Rudy
Rudy August	Breckin Rudy
Rudy William	William Rudy
Rudy Fox	Fox Rudy
Rudy Benedict	Benson Rudy

meaning

pronounced rew-dee | famous wolf
English from German
#namesdailyrudy

thank you

Stephanie, aka @anastasiaruby: Thank you for sparking my love of names out into the open. Thank you for your kindness, generosity, and authenticity. You are proof that it just takes one person giving themselves permission to set many free.

Josiah, you've pulled me outside of my comfort zone and given me a safe space to create. I've learned some things with you, like, life is just a bunch of adulting and decision-making, always make room for laughing, and breakthrough comes with breaking. You are better because of me.

But in all seriousness, Josiah is a branding mastermind. Visit his website **theNewYorkSherpa.com**

Judah + Reagan, Aaron + Andrew - you've taught me so much. I was born to be who I am because of you.

 ...and mitts off my leftovers.

Moriah Hickman + Rein Photo
 // contributing photographers

Sarah Colt @sfilly03
 // contributing artist but don't blame her for page 61

Alix Brown
 // design

If you could only sense how important you are to the lives of those you meet; how important you can be to the people you may never even dream of.

The connections we make in the course of a life - maybe that's what heaven is.

- Fred Rogers

Thank you, sweet reader, for
believing in this mama's expertise.
Whether this helped you name your
baby or is being used as a dust pan,
I think you're pretty awesome.
(unless you pronounce syrup "seerup" and then you're just pretty)

Did you like this?! ★★★★★
Share on Instagram with #namesdailybook

visit

TheNameMentor.com

for more resources

 @namesdaily

 /thenamementor

 /thenamementor

/thenamementor

From Whence I've Come

When I was a girl...

In the chilly spring nights, I had clothes laid out on a chair next to my bed ready to be thrust on at any moment. As soon as I would hear my dad's "Come on up" from my shallow sleep, I'd jump from bed and run all the way up to the barn gate where I'd pause and gently, ever so carefully, open it without the chain jingling. One light in the barn would be on and I was a moth to the flame.

You see, underneath that light was the holiness of motherhood. A birthing stall was sacred ground. Good most often comes from suffering. I remember just being tall enough to peer over into it, just for a glance. The mare sweating and biting her stomach, the panting, the making sure she was safe enough to lay in her most vulnerable state and birth her foal.

You see, "Foal watch" is a farm girl's Christmas morning.

In the dead of a night is when most foals would be born. I look back now and see how incredibly lucky I was to get to see this sight over and over. To see the bravery of motherhood crossing all different kinds of kinds. As people, we name the animals, but I've often wondered what their own mother called them in their own tongue.

Perhaps it's where I've come from that has shaped me so much for this community. Maybe that's why I hold this moment of welcoming a baby as so sacred. I never cease to be honored when asked into people's most vulnerable moment. To join them under their little light to be a voice in their quiet anticipation. I'm completely dumbfounded every time, that a lil ole farm girl like me gets to be welcomed in by all of you.

Cheers to all you mothers, of all kinds of kinds.

Alix

notes, thoughts + names you love

"Few are those who see with their own eyes
and feel with their own hearts."
- Albert Einstein